CYCLES IN NATURE

ROCK CYCLE

BY GOLRIZ GOLKAR

Kids Core
An Imprint of Abdo Publishing
abdobooks.com

abdobooks.com

Published by Abdo Publishing, a division of ABDO, PO Box 398166, Minneapolis, Minnesota 55439.

Printed in the United States of America, North Mankato, Minnesota.
102025
012026

Cover Photo: Shutterstock Images
Interior Photos: Shutterstock Images, 4–5, 7, 9, 15, 22, 25, 26, 28–29; Galyna Andrushko/Shutterstock Images, 10; Sascha Burkard/Shutterstock Images, 12–13; David Oster/Shutterstock Images, 17; Sebastian Janicki/Shutterstock Images, 18; Davide Arizzi/500px Plus/Getty Images, 20–21; Kens Canning/Shutterstock Images, 23

Editor: Trudy Becker
Series Designer: Katharine Hale

Library of Congress Control Number: 2025939315

Publisher's Cataloging-in-Publication Data

Names: Golkar, Golriz, author.
Title: Rock cycle / by Golriz Golkar
Description: Minneapolis, Minnesota: Abdo Publishing, 2026 | Series: Cycles in nature | Includes online resources and index.
Identifiers: ISBN 9781098298661 (lib. bdg.) | ISBN 9798384932468 (ebook)
Subjects: LCSH: Rocks--Juvenile literature. | Rock cycles--Juvenile literature. | Geoscience (Geology)--Juvenile literature. | Natural cycle--Juvenile literature. | Ecological processes--Juvenile literature. | Geological archaeology--Juvenile literature.
Classification: DDC 552--dc23

CONTENTS

Some science museums display rocks. People may also keep personal collections.

SPARKLING ROCKS

Sarah wanders through the science museum. Her class is on a field trip. She looks at a case of rocks on display. Three chunks of rock sit under a bright light. A shiny black rock catches her eye first. The sign says that the rock is called anthracite.

The next rock has a speckled pattern of pink, black, and white. Crystals sparkle across it in the light. The sign calls it granite. The last rock is gray with swirling patterns. This one is slate.

Sarah wants to learn more about the rocks. She walks over to a large sign on the wall. It says that all these rocks looked different in the past. Natural processes changed them over time. And their current state is not the end. The rocks will continue to change as time passes. These changes make up the rock cycle.

Sarah looks back toward the case. The slate looks familiar. She thinks she has seen it near her house. Then Sarah moves on to the next case. She can't wait to see more interesting rocks and learn how they formed.

Some beaches are lined with slate rocks.

Types of Rocks

Rocks are made of minerals. Minerals are natural substances. They do not come from animals or plants. They are found in Earth's **crust**.

There are three main kinds of rocks. One type is sedimentary rocks. These rocks form from pressed layers of **silt**, sand, dead plants, and animal skeletons. Igneous rocks are another kind. These form from melted rock deep inside Earth's crust. Metamorphic rocks are the last type. They form when pressure and heat change other kinds of rock.

Rocks and Earth's History

Rocks hold clues about Earth's past. Some rock types show that pieces of land were once underwater. Or they can show that land was under ice. Breaks in rocks can show how earthquakes moved the land. **Fossils** in sedimentary rocks can even show where and when certain plants and animals lived.

Rocks may contain records of ancient plants or animals.

Hikers can visit giant sandstone caverns in Utah.

The rock cycle does not have a set order. This means that any rock could change into another type. For example, a sedimentary rock could slowly change into a metamorphic rock. Then it could change back to sedimentary again. Some types of igneous rocks can even become other types of igneous rocks. As rocks change, Earth's surface changes too.

Further Evidence

Look at the website below. Does it give new evidence to support Chapter One?

The Rock Cycle

abdocorelibrary.com/rock-cycle

Waves can slowly wear down rock over time.

CHAPTER 2

NATURE CHANGES ROCKS

Weathering is a key part of the rock cycle. Weathering is when rocks, mud, sand, and other natural materials break down. Over time, this process creates sedimentary rock.

Rain and flowing water can cause weathering. So can wind. Temperature changes can also break down materials. For example, some rocks have water trapped inside them. When that water freezes and melts, the rocks may break up. Chemicals in the air and water are another source of weathering. In some cases, even living things such as animals and plants break down rocks.

Broken pieces of natural material are called sediment. **Erosion** often moves this material around. Water, wind, and ice may carry the sediment to other places. In some cases, sediment ends up on land. Other times, sediment builds up at the bottom of lakes, rivers, or oceans.

Breaking Down and Building Up

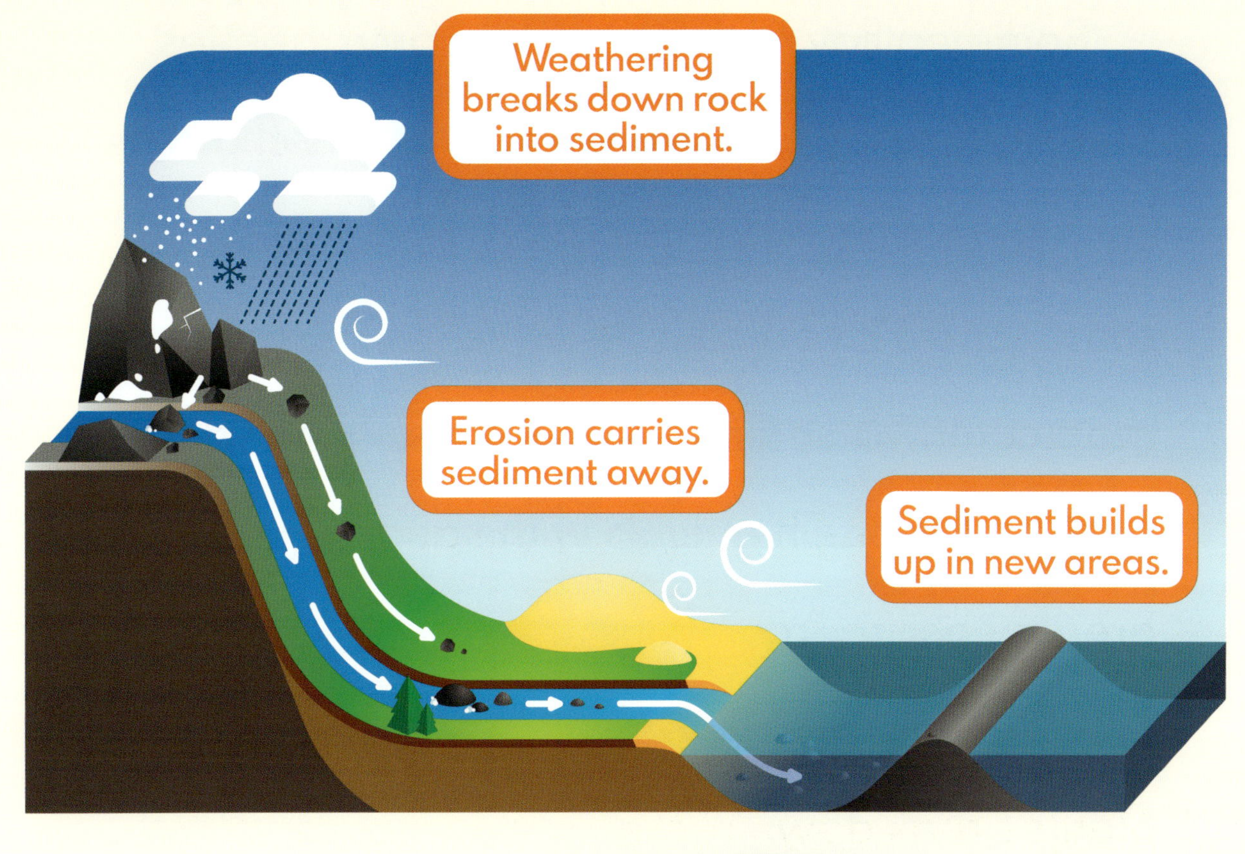

There are many ways that rocks can break down and build up in other spots.

This sediment forms thick layers. The layers get heavy over time. The weight of the top layers presses down. Then sediment further down becomes solid. It turns into sedimentary rock.

Sedimentary rock comes in many varieties. Sandstone is one example. It forms when grains of sand turn into rock. The rock can be pink, red, or gray. It can also be soft or hard. The most common sedimentary rock is shale. This gray rock is often layered with sandstone. It breaks easily.

Rock Landforms

Uluru is a giant rock **landform** in Australia. Its sandstone rock is gray. However, it looks red under sunlight. The Grand Canyon in Arizona is made of sandstone and mudstone. Mudstone is a sedimentary rock made from mud. The Grand Canyon also includes some igneous rock.

Arthur's Seat in Scotland is an inactive volcano. It contains different types of igneous rock.

Melting Rocks

A different natural process forms igneous rock. Igneous rock begins as melted rock inside Earth. The rock begins about 30 to 120 miles (50–200 km) deep. These areas are much hotter than Earth's surface. Deep inside Earth, hot gases and steam cause rocks to melt.

Next, the melted rock forms a doughlike substance. This material is called magma.

Quartz crystals can be part of sedimentary, igneous, and metamorphic rock.

Magma can erupt to Earth's surface through volcanoes. Once magma reaches the surface, it is called lava. Lava cools down on the surface. The liquid turns solid. This creates igneous rock.

Igneous rocks often include crystals. They form when lava cools slowly. These rocks may also trap gas bubbles. Pumice is an igneous rock formed from lava. The rock is gray and lightweight. Tiny crystals often cover it. Obsidian is also formed from lava. This rock is dark and shiny. However, it has no visible crystals. That is because it cools too quickly for crystals to form.

Igneous rocks formed from hot magma tend to cool slowly. Earth's inner heat slows down the cooling process. This means these rocks often have time to grow bigger crystals. Granite forms this way. Over time, it develops many colorful and shiny crystals.

Explore Online

Visit the website below. Does it give any new information about rocks that wasn't in Chapter Two?

Geology 101

abdocorelibrary.com/rock-cycle

The Marble Caves in Chile are made of metamorphic rock in many areas.

CHAPTER 3

BECOMING NEW ROCKS

Sometimes one kind of rock changes into another type of rock. New rocks formed in this way are called metamorphic rocks. Sedimentary, igneous, or other metamorphic rocks can create them.

Heat from hot rocks under Earth's surface can create geysers and hot springs.

In some cases, high heat melts down rock. This often forms igneous rock. However, in other cases, heat makes rocks compact and dense. This can happen within Earth's crust. The colors, textures, and minerals of rocks may change. The rocks are now metamorphic rocks. They have different features than before.

Metamorphic rocks may also form from pressure. Rocks inside Earth's crust may be pressed down, broken up, or even folded. Sometimes, the movement of Earth's **tectonic plates** causes this. Plates move slowly along Earth's surface. When two plates crash together, it creates heat and strong pressure.

The movements of tectonic plates can create mountain ranges.

The movement can break and fold enormous pieces of rock and land. It can even form new mountains.

Forming Something New

Gneiss is a common metamorphic rock. It is made from both sedimentary and igneous rocks. Gneiss often forms from granite that was

Uses of Rocks

Rocks are a key **natural resource**. Soil is made up of weathered rocks. Soil helps plants grow. Other rocks, such as limestone, granite, and sandstone, are common building materials. And many rocks contain precious minerals and stones. People can get gold, silver, and diamonds from them.

The Parthenon is an ancient temple of the Greek goddess Athena. It is made of marble.

exposed to high temperatures and pressures. Gneiss tends to have stripes from folding. Marble is also metamorphic. It forms when limestone is exposed to heat and pressure. Marble is often gray and white. It may even include swirls of red, white, or blue.

People burn rocks such as coal to make energy.

Metamorphic rocks may also undergo changes. Weathering can break the rocks down into sedimentary rocks. Through melting and cooling, they may become igneous rocks. Other types of rocks go through changes as well. As time passes, they move back and forth through different phases of the rock cycle. Earth's rocks are always changing.

PRIMARY SOURCE

Scientist Alan Cutler discussed the rock cycle. He said:

> The rock cycle has no set time frame. That is, the stages . . . can occur over time scales ranging from very short (days, or even less) to very long (billions of years).

Source: Alan H. Cutler. "Steno and the Rock Cycle." *Substantia*, vol. 5, no. 1, 2021, fupress.com. Accessed 3 June 2025.

Comparing Texts

Think about the quote. Does it support the information in this chapter? Or does it give a different perspective? Explain how in a few sentences.

CYCLE SUMMARY

Cooling

Heat and pressure

Igneous rock

Weathering and erosion

Weathering and erosion

Sediment

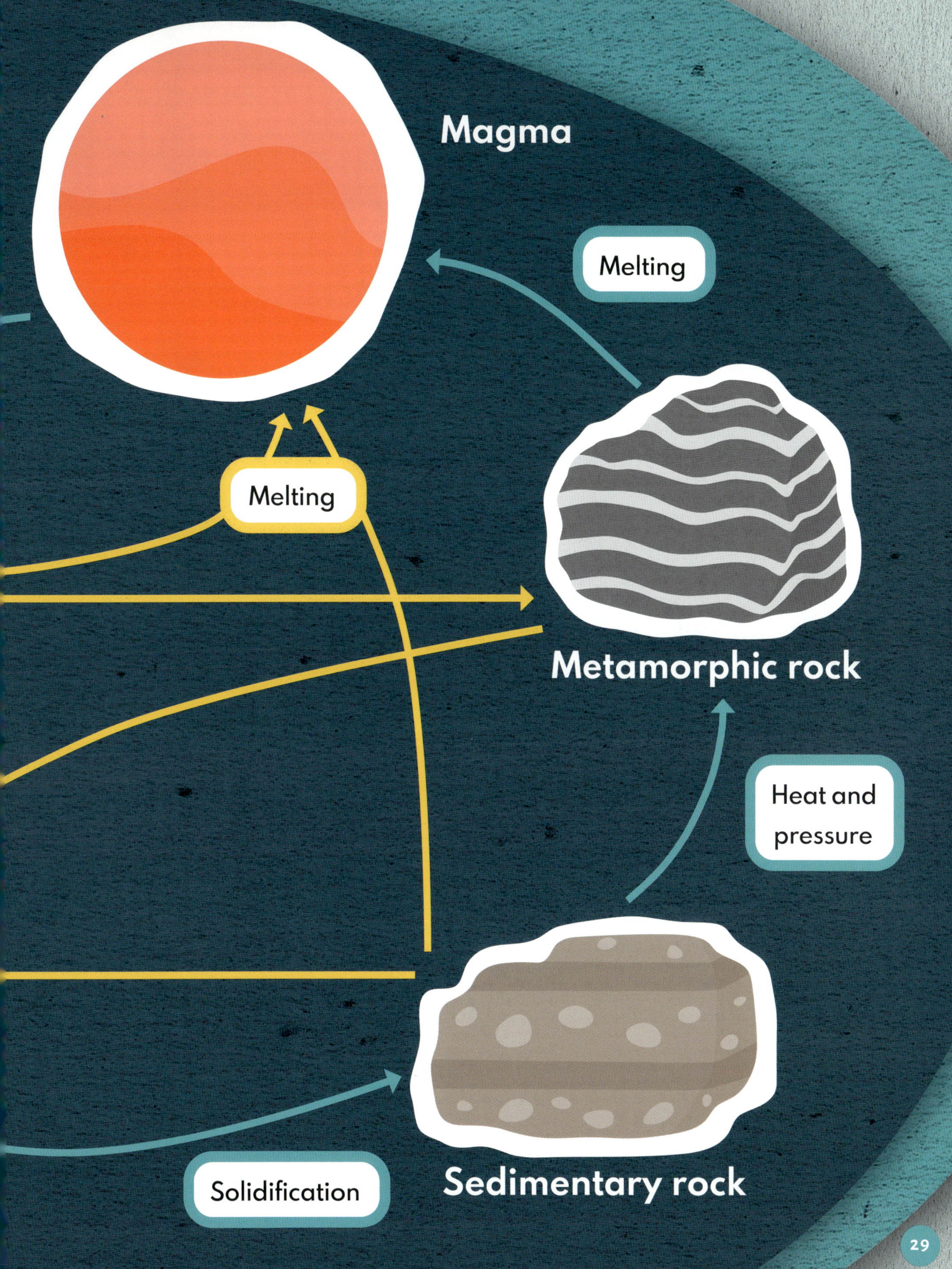
Magma
Melting
Melting
Metamorphic rock
Heat and pressure
Sedimentary rock
Solidification

Glossary

crust
the outer layer of Earth

erosion
the process of land being moved or broken down by water, wind, and ice

fossils
the remains of very old plants or animals that are preserved in rock

landform
a naturally formed rock structure on Earth's surface

natural resource
something found in nature that people can use

silt
very fine soil that is carried by water

tectonic plates
massive pieces of rock that make up Earth's crust

Online Resources

To learn more about the rock cycle, visit our free resource websites below.

Visit **abdocorelibrary.com** or scan this QR code for free Common Core resources for teachers and students, including vetted activities, multimedia, and booklinks, for deeper subject comprehension.

Visit **abdobooklinks.com** or scan this QR code for free additional online weblinks for further learning. These links are routinely monitored and updated to provide the most current information available.

Learn More

Gieseke, Tyler. *The Rock Cycle.* Abdo, 2023.

Murray, Julie. *Minerals.* Abdo, 2025.

Murray, Julie. *Rocks.* Abdo, 2025.

Index

About the Author

Golriz Golkar has written more than 100 nonfiction and fiction books for children. She holds a BA in American literature and culture from UCLA and an EdM in language and literacy from the Harvard Graduate School of Education. Golriz lives in France with her husband and young daughter.